LEARN HOW TO PROTECT YOUR IDEA AND MAKE IT PROFITABLE

MW01051397

TABLE OF CONTENTS

"Invention strictly speaking, is little more than a new combination of those images which have been previously gathered and deposited in the memory; nothing can come from nothing."

- Sir Joshua Reynolds

INTRODUCTION

I want to offer this eBook as a practical guide and help to amateur inventors and beginners in the field of technical creativity. Words "amateur" and "beginner" do not indicate person's age by any mean. Through years of my technical and creative career I discovered, that "invention bug" bites people of all and any genders, ages and races. It is really a bug, a disease, if you want. I never saw an inventor, a person who invented something once and stopped, never trying to invent again... and again.

In this book reader will find general guidelines about protecting an idea as well as detailed step-by-step instructions on how to apply for provisional patent without hiring patent attorney. Patenting process in general may be very complicated and cumbersome, so, I cannot say that services of good patent attorney are unnecessary. In some, if not most, situations, hiring patent attorney is a must, if you are serious about your invention. But many initial steps can be done by the inventor him/her-self, saving time and money.

This is my first edition of the book for amateur and beginner inventors, which was prompted for creation by many meetings with people, who were calling me or coming into my office and asking for help with their ideas. Were all these ideas great? No, of course, not all of them were ingenious. But most of the ideas brought by amateur inventors were truly great, smart, fresh and potentially very useful and promising to become very practical.

The biggest problem with these visits for me was in the fact, that I was and still am running business and cannot afford to spend too much of my time without being paid. Unfortunately, most of the amateur inventors do not come from rich families or have sponsors and investors, backing them up financially. The process of invention and protecting an idea is not coming cheap either. Inventors must run research and build rough and not-so-rough prototypes. Patent attorneys, like all of their kind, charge top dollars for their services. Many inventors are not engineers themselves and often do not have knowledge of design, engineering, manufacturing and marketing. All of the above and many other factors pushed me towards decision to write a short book, which would help inventors to understand some of the most important points and steps in the process of inventing, protecting and marketing their ideas and in making an educated decision about how to monetize on their inventions, while minimizing risks of having their valuable ideas stolen.

G. I. Fedorov
Newton, New Jersey
December 11, 2015

ABOUT THE AUTHOR

Gennadi Fedorov is a designer and inventor, author of 14 issued and current US utility patents and several patents pending. He is also founder and chief designer of Atus Design, LLC., a successful design consultancy with offices in Newton, New Jersey. He has over 25 years of experience in the fields of industrial design, consumer product design, engineering and manufacturing. He received Master's

Degree in Industrial and Product Design in 1991 from Stiglitz' Academy of Design in St. Petersburg, Russia.

"You have to learn the rules of the game. And then you have to play better than anyone else."
- Albert Einstein

BASIC INFORMATION ABOUT US PATENTING SYSTEM

On March 16, 2013 the U.S. adopted "first-to-file" system, which means that if you filed patent application first, you will be considered the inventor, no matter how long someone else had this idea.

Everything evolves and changes and so does the patent system in the USA and patent systems around the world. This book is encompassing general information, which is current at the moment of writing, but most likely, book will have to be updated from time to time to reflect changes in US patenting laws, regulations and practices. Until 2013 US patent system was giving authorship rights to inventor who could prove that he had idea first, even though he may not have been the first to apply for a patent for this idea. On March 16, 2013 system changed and a "first-to-file" system was adopted, which means that inventor who filed for the patent first would be considered the inventor, no matter how long ago someone else had this idea.

US Patenting System does not make any distinction whatsoever between inventors, who are US citizen or foreigners, residing in US or their home countries or elsewhere in the world.

Inventors for many years were using different methods for recording their inventions and ideas without patenting them, hoping one day to use recorded and proven dates to claim priority rights. Some believed that sending sketches and descriptions to one-self by registered mail and then keeping packet unopened will provide proof of priority in court if it ever comes to that. Others were regularly visiting local banks or notary offices and stamping their notes with dates and notary stamps and signatures. None of this works any longer. Now, if you have an idea, apply for a patent or risk losing it. Simple, square and fair.

The America Invents Act passed On September 12, 2011, the "America Invents Act" was adopted, which stipulates, that any public sale or disclosure prior to filing a patent application will jeopardize your ability to obtain patent protection.

SO, YOU THINK YOU HAVE A GREAT IDEA! NOW WHAT?

First, you need to perform certain steps trying to find out if your idea is unique and has not been invented previously. In patent language this is called "Prior Art". This means thorough combing through available patent information. This is a strange job, where you do not want to find any prior art relating to your idea, but at the same time you have to be very tedious in searching for it. How odd, isn't it? But proper and thorough search may save you a lot of frustration, time, energy and money in a long run. So, again, there is just no way around this. You must try to be as un-biased towards your own idea as possible. Is this even possible? Probably not... It is like asking a loving parent to stop adoring his/her child so much. Inventors often start sharing their idea with their family members and close friends and asking their opinion. Usually, this results in very positive and encouraging reviews, which are more often than not far from being objective and constructive. So, what is the first step in determining if your idea has any real potential and real value? The answer is - PATENT RESEARCH! And thanks God for the Internet! Researching the Web can provide most, if not all, answers to these questions.

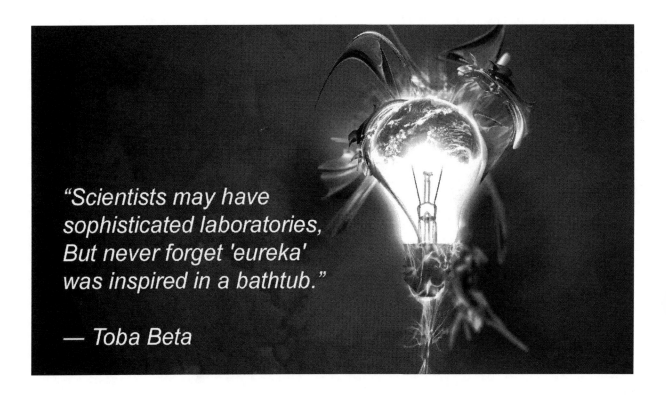

"Scientists may have sophisticated laboratories, But never forget 'eureka' was inspired in a bathtub."

— Toba Beta

WHAT IS PROVISIONAL UTILITY PATENT APPLICATION?

There are several types of patents and patent applications, but we will concentrate mostly on one of them – utility patent application, specifically on Provisional Patent Application, often referred to as PPA. Provisional Patent Application system was introduced in US in 1994 as a mean to make it easier for independent inventors and small companies to apply for patent for their ideas, enabling them to obtain protection and ways to more securely market these ideas. PPA is a lot cheaper and simpler than non-

PPA and it provides an inventor 12 months of protection for the idea and official "patent pending" status. This makes it somewhat easier and more secure process of marketing and selling idea, if inventor is intent on doing that. Within this 12-months period inventor can develop and attempt to pitch and sell his idea to potential buyers or prepare to manufacture it himself.

Another important detail about PPA is that for its filing inventor may, but does not have to include claims for his invention. Sketches or drawings, accompanied by a description, simple form and small payment is all that is needed to submit PPA. And application can be submitted either on paper by regular mail or electronically through USPTO web system. As of March 19, 2013 USPTO provides inventors submitting PPA with an opportunity to pay reduced filing fees if applicant meets qualifications as Small Entity or Micro Entity. Small Entity pays $130 per PPA, Micro Entity is required to pay only $65. This was done to provide a break to smaller companies and independent individual inventors and support creative innovation.

APPLICATION FEE TABLE:

Definition of Entity	Class of Entity	PPA Filing Fees
Companies with over 500 employees	Large Entity	$260
Individual or small company with more than $161,000 annual gross income and less than 500 employees	Small Entity	$130
Entities with gross annual income of $160,971 or less; other requirements apply.	Micro Entity	$65

More current and updated filing fees may be verified by visiting USPTO website:
http://www.uspto.gov/learning-and-resources/fees-and-payment/uspto-fee-schedule

Please, be aware that if you qualify as Small or Micro Entity, but are planning or obligated to assign patent rights to a larger company, which does not qualify for these categories, then you cannot claim Small or Micro Entity status. Doing so improperly may result in loss of patent rights. It is important also to fully understand that PPA is not a patent and not even a full non-Provisional Application. If PPA is not converted into a non-Provisional Application within 12-months period, inventor may lose any right to patent his idea. This all may sound a bit more complicated and more confusing than it really is. Just read on…

CONS AND PROS OF PROVISIONAL PATENT APPLICATION

As you make your research about Provisional Patent Applications you will find a lot of information about this topic and a lot off offers of services, ranging from $1000's in costs from large law firms to $99 per application promising "patent pending" status within 12 hours. They often advertise their services with a phrase "Provisional Patent Application Made easy!" While it is true – provisional patent application is considerably easier and cheaper than non-provisional application, it is extremely important to understand what exactly it does for you. It is important to realize, that taking provisional application too easy, "cutting corners" in preparing its description and drawings may render the whole idea of application useless. Any detail about your invention, that you may omit or miss in your description will not be considered part of that invention, so, it is extremely important to pay serious attention to writing detailed and proper description for your invention in provisional patent application. This especially true, because patent claims in provisional patent application are not required. So, if you do not have claims, only description and drawings can show details of your invention and point out what the novelty is in your idea. If you skip on description and provide un-clear drawings, your whole application can either be rendered useless or it may be easily bypassed by someone with a better understanding how to prepare drawings and description and in case of non-provisional patent application – claims. So, my resume of this paragraph is this – provisional patent application is a tremendous help provided to independent inventors by USPTO, but it must be understood well and used properly and wisely.

SEARCHING GOOGLE

Google and WWW these days are like an ocean. It is great to come to swim and catch a fish or two. But it is also quite easy to drown, if you are not watchful, selective and careful. When you will start your search on Google, you will inevitably come across overwhelming number of search results with advises ranging from "Do All Of It Yourself!" to "Do Not Attempt To Do It Without a Professional Help". There will be success stories and scary failure stories. The truth, as it is in most cases, lays somewhere in a middle. Trust your own life experience and intuition. This book is no exception. If you do not trust my book, do not use it as your guide. Find a source that gives you more confidence.

I would recommend to start your patent research from Google. First, search existing products using different terms describing your idea. Just think of your invention and try to find different terms and phrases that may describe it and run them through Google in conjunction with word PATENT. In many cases your results will show different patent sources and web publications. If your idea is for a physical object, a consumer or commercial product, it may make a lot of sense to start an "easy" search first – through Google images. Internet these days is full of pictures of products and their descriptions, so, Google image search may often reveal if your idea already exists in a form of product or not.

You need to understand that if product already exists, you most likely cannot apply for a patent that describes it, even if there is no previously issued patent for that product. Objects, which are available to everybody are in so called "Public Domain" and cannot be patented, unless you create a smart enough improvement or modification that can be considered innovative enough to secure a patent.

*You need to understand and differentiate from two possible publications – **issued patents** and **published patent applications**. The difference is simple – issued patents are documents that have been approved and issued and which grant status of patent to an invention with a list of accepted claims. These claims describe exactly what is protected in the patent as novelty. Published application is not a patent yet. It may or may not be granted, but at least it provides a basic understanding, that someone had an idea and tries to protect it.*

Some of the discovered publications will be in webpage formats, other may come up as PDF files. There is no way around this – you must open them one by one and read titles and at least few lines of description. Some publications will offer to view drawings. If you did not find patents or published applications relating to your invention, this is a first good sign, indicating that your idea may not have been invented. Not yet. But there is quite a bit more work and research left to be done. It makes a lot of sense to invest you time and energy in patent research to make sure that your idea is indeed unique. Further steps may require that you invest some money. By thorough initial patent research you make sure that your additional time and money will be well spent.

SEARCHING USPTO DATABASE

Next step in running a thorough search on USPTO website. Go to http://patft.uspto.gov/ will bring you to the search portal of USPTO database. First, let's understand what options are available to you on this page. Below is a snapshot of the webpage which will become your USPTO database search starting point. Middle column contains links to information explaining how to use search feature on USPTO, how database structured and other useful information. You will learn a lot if you take time and browse this section. If only to know where to go when you come across a difficulty with your search. Column on the left side provides search options to search issued patents. Column on the right provides similar tools to search published patent applications. Column in a middle provides explanations on how to use search tools of USPTO database. I encourage you to read its sections before running your search. This may prevent misunderstanding and may save you a lot of time and frustration in a long run.

PatFT: Patents
Full-Text from 1976

Quick Search
Advanced Search
Number Search

View Full-Page Images

PatFT Help Files
PatFT Status, History
PatFT Database Contents

Report Problems

<< BOTH SYSTEMS >>

The databases are operating normally.

Notices & Policies

How to View Images

Assignment Database

Public PAIR

Searching by Class

Sequence Listings

Attorneys and Agents

Privacy Policy

AppFT: Applications
Published since March 2001

Quick Search
Advanced Search
Number Search

View Full-Page Images

AppFT Help Files
AppFT Status, History

Report Problems

Be aware that if searching applications (right column of screenshot above) did not produce any result, this may still not mean that there is no previously filed applications that could prevent you from filing yours. Currently, average time from time of filing a patent application to its publication on USPTO is around one year or more.

Newer computers should not have problem to view full-page images with drawings that accompany patents and applications. If your computer does not show drawings when you click on the link "IMAGES", you need to go to "How to View Images" link in the middle column and follow information provided there to set up your computer properly. You may be required to download plugins to be able to view drawings on USPTO web database.

Here is a small example of searching USPTO database and using some available options. For example, you came up with an idea for a novelty (in your humble opinion) of a dough cutting and molding tool and need to see if there is any prior art, related to your great idea (Oh gosh... how you hope that there is none!). So, we open USPTO search page http://patft.uspto.gov , click "Quick Search" in the top of left column and type "dough" as TERM 1 and "cutter" as TERM 2 and click "Search" button or hit enter on your keyboard.

Query [Help]

Term 1: `dough`   in **Field 1:** `All Fields ▼`

`AND ▼`

Term 2: `cutter`   in **Field 2:** `All Fields ▼`

Select years [Help]

`1976 to present [full-text] ▼`   `Search` `Reset`

Few moments later we see that we have 1,496 search results. Seems quite discouraging, right? We start reading titles of the issued patents and soon realize that most of the result have to do a lot with molecular biology, nuclear physics, medical formulas and pharmaceutical and pharmacological blends and potion. To save time and avoid digging through too much un-related to our interest data we need to narrow down our search parameters. Since our tool is related to kitchen and also performs molding or forming dough, we will try to add these terms one at a time to search string. On results page it is located right above search results list:

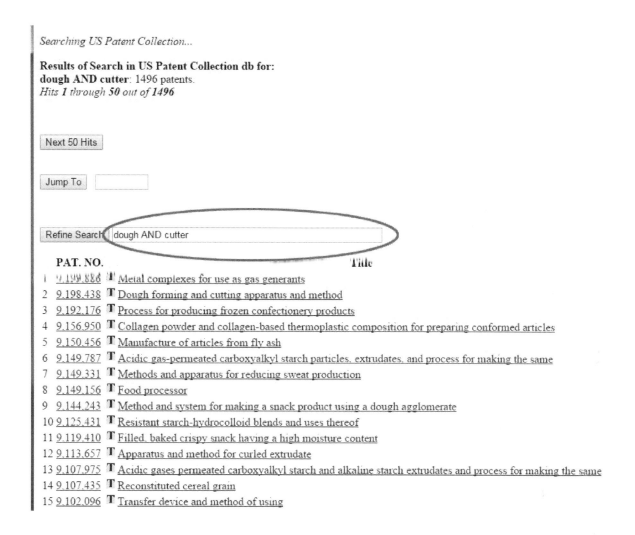

Searching US Patent Collection...

Results of Search in US Patent Collection db for:
dough AND cutter: 1496 patents.
Hits 1 through 50 out of 1496

Next 50 Hits

Jump To

Refine Search | dough AND cutter

PAT. NO.		Title
1	9,199,888	Metal complexes for use as gas generants
2	9,198,438	Dough forming and cutting apparatus and method
3	9,192,176	Process for producing frozen confectionery products
4	9,156,950	Collagen powder and collagen-based thermoplastic composition for preparing conformed articles
5	9,150,456	Manufacture of articles from fly ash
6	9,149,787	Acidic gas-permeated carboxyalkyl starch particles, extrudates, and process for making the same
7	9,149,331	Methods and apparatus for reducing sweat production
8	9,149,156	Food processor
9	9,144,243	Method and system for making a snack product using a dough agglomerate
10	9,125,431	Resistant starch-hydrocolloid blends and uses thereof
11	9,119,410	Filled, baked crispy snack having a high moisture content
12	9,113,657	Apparatus and method for curled extrudate
13	9,107,975	Acidic gases permeated carboxyalkyl starch and alkaline starch extrudates and process for making the same
14	9,107,435	Reconstituted cereal grain
15	9,102,096	Transfer device and method of using

Notice that there is a word AND in capital letters appearing between our two key words used on previous screen. This means, that system found and showed patents which have these **both** words in the patent. These keywords are not necessarily positioned next to each other and in the same order, but these both words are present somewhere in the patent text. Now, let's try to narrow down our search by adding more search terms by typing "AND" + space + "molding" and clicking "Refine Search" button or hitting Enter on the keyboard. Now we received 272 search results back:

Searching US Patent Collection...

Results of Search in US Patent Collection db for:
((dough AND cutter) AND molding): 272 patents.
Hits 1 through 50 out of 272

[Next 50 Hits]

[Jump To] [   ]

[Refine Search] dough AND cutter AND molding

PAT. NO.	Title
1 9.156.950	T Collagen powder and collagen-based thermoplastic composition for preparing conformed articles
2 9.125.431	T Resistant starch-hydrocolloid blends and uses thereof
3 9.102.096	T Transfer device and method of using
4 9.101.158	T Application of soybean emulsion composition to soybean-derived raw material-containing food or beverage
5 9.060.531	T Laminated baked snack bar
6 9.033.693	T Unitary elastic mold and cutter combination
7 9.017.752	T Shortening composition
8 8.993.504	T Oxidation catalyst for bleaching, and bleaching composition using the same
9 8.993.039	T Fiber-containing carbohydrate composition
10 8.960.836	T Image registration on edible substrates
11 8.936.461	T Transfer device and method of using
12 8.916.224	T Production of shredded or flaked whole grain-containing composite food products
13 8.882.488	T Combined stamping and cutting device for modeling compound
14 8.752.558	T Apparatus and method for forming and packaging molded tobacco pieces

That's a lot better and easier to deal with, correct? Still, results have a lot of patents not relating to your idea.

SEARCHING CROSS-REFERENCED PATENTS

Now, let's click on one of the patent titles, which sounds like it is related to our search. Clicking on result # 13 with patent # 8,882,488 "Combined stamping and cutting device for modeling compound" opens patent page that contains text but does not show drawings yet. We see button "Images" in the top section of the screen. Clicking on it will bring you to the screen where you will be able to read patent and see related drawings. But do not rush to press it yet.

USPTO PATENT FULL-TEXT AND IMAGE DATABASE

| Home | Quick | Advanced | Pat Num | Help |
| HR List | Next List | Previous | Next | Bottom |

View Cart | Add to Cart

Images

(13 of 272)

| United States Patent | 8,882,488 |
| Schultheis , et al. | November 11, 2014 |

Combined stamping and cutting device for modeling compound

Abstract

A combined toy which simply yet uniquely stamps and cuts off formed articles in a fun and interesting way utilizing cooperating rollers which employ a stamp and at least one angular projection defining a cutting edge on at least one roller. Two or more cooperating rollers are at a frame with each roller including a peripheral surface, one or more concentric ribs on the peripheral surface of each roller which cooperate to spiral around the length of each roller defining a *molding* surface which spirals around the peripheral surface of each roller, and a stamp on the *molding* surface of at least one roller. The driving mechanism rotates a gear mechanism which in turn rotates the two or more rollers that cooperate to stamp and cut off articles formed on the *molding* surface of the rollers.

Inventors:	Schultheis; Douglas Arthur (Cumberland, RI), Aust; Ashley (Providence, RI)
Applicant:	Name	City	State Country Type
	Schultheis; Douglas Arthur	Cumberland	RI	US
	Aust; Ashley	Providence	RI	US
Assignee:	Hasbro, Inc. (Pawtucket, RI)
Family ID:	49291671
Appl. No.:	13/442,461
Filed:	April 9, 2012

Prior Publication Data

| Document Identifier | Publication Date |
| US 20130264740 A1 | Oct 10, 2013 |

Scroll down a bit. You will see a section called "References Cited" and a list of patents and published applications which one way or another are related to the one we are on.

Prior Publication Data

| Document Identifier | Publication Date |
| US 20130264740 A1 | Oct 10, 2013 |

Current U.S. Class:	425/332; 264/163; 366/81; 366/85; 425/204; 425/294; 425/296; 425/333
Current CPC Class:	A63H 33/001 (20130101); B29C 47/30 (20130101); B29C 47/0002 (20130101); B29C 47/40 (20130101)
Current International Class:	B28B 1/00 (20060101)
Field of Search:	;425/204,294,296,332,333 ;264/163 ;221/30 ;366/85,81

References Cited [Referenced By]

U.S. Patent Documents

1164718	December 1915	Hill
1753834	April 1930	Ponisch
2213784	September 1940	Landow
2259623	October 1941	Dieckmann
D183650	October 1958	Gaston
D199249	September 1964	Barlow
3171636	March 1965	Barlow et al.
3496262	February 1970	Long et al.
3536014	October 1970	Kucheris
3572259	March 1971	Hayashi
3817498	June 1974	Frankfurth et al.
3892510	July 1975	Meth et al.
3899275	August 1975	Atwood
3937314	February 1976	Rosenberg et al.
4076476	February 1978	Ventura
D268043	February 1983	Orenstein
4469476	September 1984	Cavanagh et al.
4560086	December 1985	Stol
4569813	February 1986	Rentz et al.

These are all cross-referenced publications. Very helpful tool because it allows you to more quickly find closely related inventions. Scroll all the way down and start opening referenced publications from the bottom. This is because more recent patents and applications are located at the bottom of the list. If you see patent numbers that consist of 7 digits, these are issued patents. If there are more than 7 digits in a number, it is published application and not necessarily a patent yet. Each of them also may have a list of cross-referenced patents and applications. Take your time and dig through. And yes, patent search is hard labor and feels like a full-time job.

HOW TO READ PATENTS AND PUBLISHED APPLICATIONS?

Reading patents and published patent applications throughout is a good thing but takes a lot of time. Drawings, that accompany issued patents or published applications, help a lot, but you must know certain parts of these publications where you have to pay particular attention to details. Most important part of any patent is its **claims** section, which is usually located closer towards the end of the patent and starts as new paragraph with words "What is claimed is:" or "What is claimed:" or "The invention claimed is:" Reading claims carefully is the key to understanding what exactly is protected in any given patent or what is intended for protection in applications. You may find a patent directly relating to your idea, but if a feature which is unique in your invention is not claimed in issued patent, you may still have a chance to claim it and obtain your own patent. So, just finding directly related patent and description is not always the end of it. You must carefully read and understand the claims.

WHAT IS EPO AND SHOULD YOU SEARCH IT TOO?

EPO stands for European Patent Office. There is a web database where you can search for patents issued as protection in Europe https://www.epo.org/searching.html .

Do you have to search EPO as well? This depends on you and your intentions. If you believe that your idea is indeed great and unique and if you plan to apply for international protection through EPC (European Patent Convention), then it makes sense to run patent research on EPO database too. If you think, that protection of your idea only on American market is more than enough for you, why bother with EPO? However, you have to know that European patenting system is in certain ways different than US system. For example, you may have an idea, present it in a form of model or prototype during trade show or even start running production and only then decide that you want to obtain patent for it. This is still possible in the U.S., but not in Europe. In most European countries if you made any non-confidential introduction of your invention to general public before applying for patent, you automatically lose any chance to patent this idea. It becomes non-patentable public domain.

LEARN HOW TO PROTECT YOUR IDEA AND MAKE IT PROFITABLE

Home → Searching for patents

Searching for patents

Start searching
→ European patent register
→ European publication server
→ Espacenet - worldwide patent search
→ GPI - advanced search
→ Patent translate

→ **More online searching**

Before you search
→ Search essentials
→ Patent information tour

Data from the EPO

Database collections
→ Patent information services for experts
→ Subscription databases

Raw data
→ Raw data download area
→ About raw data products and sample data

About EPO data
→ Latest patent additions
→ Latest full-text additions
→ Useful tables and statistics

Asian patent information

Virtual helpdesk
Help with patent information from:
→ China
→ Chinese Taipei
→ India
→ Japan
→ Korea

Other services
→ Search services
→ Translation services

→ **All services**

Upcoming events

15.12.2015 | Virtual classroom, online
Global Patent Index (GPI) Advanced

11.1.2016 | Virtual classroom, online
Patent information user support bi-monthly webinars

18.1.2016 | Virtual classroom, online
Legal status

→ **All events**

Website updates

10.12.2015
EPO offices closed from 24.12.2015 to 3.1.2016

25.11.2015
Temporary unavailability of online services on 28 November 2015

19.11.2015
Temporary unavailability of online services on 21 November 2015

12.11.2015
Temporary unavailability of online services on 14 November 2015

12.11.2015
Temporary unavailability of online services on 15 November 2015

5.11.2015
Temporary unavailability of online services on 8 November 2015

2.11.2015
Unavailability of some web services on 7 November 2015

19.10.2015
Temporary unavailability of online services on 25 October 2015

→ Updates archive
RSS: patent information

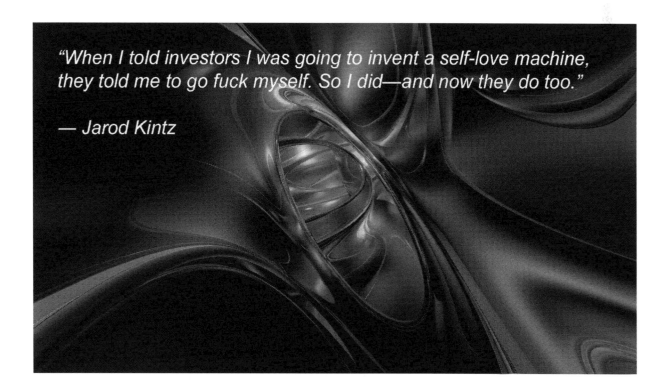

"When I told investors I was going to invent a self-love machine, they told me to go fuck myself. So I did—and now they do too."

— Jarod Kintz

PUBWEST AND PUBEAST. WHAT ARE THESE?

EAST stands for Examiner's Automated Search Tool and WEST stands for Web-based Examiner's Search Tool. These are a bit too specific to be used by amateur inventors and in many cases not needed. I provide just factual information about these tools, but we will not be covering them in this book.

NO PRIOR ART! WHAT DOES THIS MEAN?

Phrase "Prior Art" is a fancy phrase that simply means "previously issued patents or published applications". If you performed Google search and USPTO search and they did not reveal any patent or application that relates directly to your idea, this is normally a very good sign. This means, that so far you did not find any "Prior Art". It is hard to say how long one should spend searching for signs of prior art. On some projects I was spending between 4 to 6 days painstakingly combing USPTO database and other on-line resources just to make sure that I am not "inventing a wheel". On others it could take me as little as 3-4 hours of research to understand that my idea was unique enough and I can go ahead with developing it into a product. Searching USPTO is a hard job, but in many instances you come across patents, which may give you even better ideas for improving your own.

So, no prior art. Now we can start planning product development and deciding what to do with our idea – sell it, license it or make it. Product development process most often requires that you share your idea with someone else – prototype maker, design consultant, marketing people. At this point protection of your idea is the most important step. You have to protect your idea ASAP. This involves two steps. One – obtaining and using NDA (Non-Disclosure Agreement) any time you have to speak with someone professionally about your idea. NDA is not all-around protection, but it gives you a piece of mind and implies that person or company which is involved in discussions of your idea takes certain responsibility to keep your idea confidential and not use or disclose it to someone else without consulting you first. Second step is preparing and filing a provisional patent application. In some case you may want or need a professional help even to start preparing for provisional patent application – making sketches, drawings, graphs or building models and prototypes. Make sure that you have them sign NDA before opening any discussion. Most design, engineering and marketing consultants have generic blank NDA ready to be signed. Just ask them about it. If they send it to you, read it all before signing and ask them any questions about points which are unclear. You can review and use generic NDA form posted in "Forms And Examples" section in the end of this book. Usually, generic NDA is one or two pages long. We will cover this topic in more details later.

If you are from rich family or have huge income yourself, you are in good shape and do not need this book and anybody's advice. You should simply find a good patent attorney and hire him/her to do patent research and patent application for you. Most patent attorneys have connections with artists who create drawings for patent applications. And if you have no problem with money, you may even decide to skip provisional application and go straight to full non-provisional utility patent application. Unfortunately, most of independent inventors are not rich enough for these steps and have to do a lot of work themselves. This is when an opportunity to start with provisional patent application comes very handy.

While cost of provisional patent application is more or less known: $260 for "normal" application; $130 per application for Small Entity and $65 for Micro Entity, cost of non-provisional application is not so defined and depends on several factors. Average cost of non-provisional patent application varies between $12,000 and $20,000, including attorney's fees.

WRITING AND FILING PROVISIONAL PATENT APPLICATION

We will start with a short and simple checklist of what you need to have prepared for filing provisional patent application:

- Drawing(s) and/or sketch(es) or chart(s) of your idea. See example at the end of this book.
- Description of your invention. You can view example at the end of the book:
- Provisional Application Cover Sheet Form PTO/SB/16
- Application filing fee; $130 if you are a Small Entity; $65 if you are Micro Entity.

When your application is ready it can be filed either on-line at USPTO website, which is very easy and fast. In that case you will need to use your credit card to make payment of filing fees. Or, you can print out your documents, include filing fees in a form of check, certified check or money order written to **Director of the U.S. Patent and Trademark Office** and mail everything to the following address:

Commissioner for Patents
P.O. Box 1450
Alexandria, VA 22313-1450

Detailed information about preparing and submitting provisional patent application may be obtained at USPTO website here:

http://www.uspto.gov/patents-getting-started/patent-basics/types-patent-applications/provisional-application-patent

You can print all required parts of PPA on paper and send it by mail. If you prefer to file your PPA on-line electronically, USPTO offers EFS-Web (Electronic Filing System) for this specific purpose. You can learn more about EFS-Web here: http://www.uspto.gov/patents/process/file/efs/guidance.

On my blog http://www.myinventionhub.com I had created a section named "Useful Links" where I collected and referenced web resources with information related to patenting topics, where you can find this and additional free information, useful links, free forms and examples.

PATENT APPLICATION DRAWINGS

In the list of documents required for filing Provisional Patent Application I put drawings as the first requirement. There is a reason for that. Drawings and description are closely connected with each other. You write your description, while referring to parts of your drawings, this is why you start with preparing drawings first and then go on working on description. You can provide as many drawings as you want or need with your application, but remember that more drawings do not necessarily mean better application and better protection. You may submit only one sketch with your application, if it illustrates your unique idea clear enough. If you invented a new product and it contains two or more parts, you have to come up with a name for each part and create references to each part. Make sure that you do not modify part name in your description.

There is a very helpful trick for assigning numbers to the parts in your drawing(s): Start with assigning "1" to any part of your drawing and then use only odd numbers: "3", "5", "7", etc. By "missing" every other number you give yourself a chance to use them later on and add numbered references if needed.

Provisional Patent Application does not require to include claims with your description. Claims must be part of Non-Provisional Patent Application. Writing good claims is a skill, which is harder and trickier than it may seem. Good drawings and proper description is all you need for now. Your drawing(s) must illustrate your unique idea in a most clear way possible. And your description must do the same using words. At the end of this book in "Forms and Examples" section you will find an example of description and drawings with numbered references for provisional patent application.

SHOULD YOU CONSIDER PROTECTING YOUR IDEA GLOBALLY?

Global protection is a serious matter to think about, but you have up to 12 months to make that decision, when you will be ready to turn your PPA application into Non-PPA. At the moment you just need to know that you will have this option to protect your idea on a global market by submitting PCT (Patent Cooperation Treaty) application with USPTO. Currently, some 148 countries are members of this treaty. Some ideas are worth spending additional money and protecting globally. If you are independent inventor with limited funds, you need to consider this –US market alone may be large enough for your product and you do not need to worry about protecting it elsewhere.

In case you are not sure or consider possibility in the near future to extend protection for your idea globally, please, make sure that any disclosure of this idea is made confidentially. If you post your idea on public YouTube cannel, discussion forum or any other public-accessible Internet website, or if you exhibit drawings and prototypes in a trade show, this will be considered public exposure and may greatly limit your ability to obtain patent protection for your idea.

Most European countries have laws which disallow any patent protection for ideas which have been disclosed publically prior to date of filing PCT application.

MAKING DECISION: SELL, LICENSE OR MANUFACTURE?

You have finally filed your PPA and your idea is now officially "patent pending". It is time to start thinking about your next steps. There are three major options to consider and to choose from:

1. Develop a product, make it and sell it on your own through distribution and/or retail.
2. Sell your idea to a firm, which is operates in the field, to which your invention belongs.
3. License right to manufacture product, based on your idea to a firm or corporation.

The choice is tough and each of the three options have CON's and PRO's. I am not giving here any particular preference for any of the three ways to handle monetization from your idea. This decision must be made based on particular details and circumstances of every inventor's case individually. One thing all three options above have in common, though. It is pitching your idea. This means preparation of good presentation by building models and/or working prototypes, preparing presentation boards and market and cost analysis charts.

MANUFACTURING: WHAT YOU NEED TO KNOW

Manufacturing on your own may potentially be more financially rewarding in some unforeseeable future, but it also means more responsibility, a lot of very hard work, and, what in most inventors' cases is very important, - considerably more money to invest. Product development, prototyping, testing, possibly safety certifications, tooling, sourcing, manufacturing, freight, warehousing and other overhead expenses – this is just a short list of where you will have to put a lot of money before you will see any signs of return on your investments. Most of the time independent inventors can afford this avenue only when they get lucky to find investors. Yet, you will still need a good presentation to convince potential partner to put money into your business. This also means signing a serious partnership agreement or few, which is very hard to do right without help of a good (and most likely expensive) attorney.

LICENSING YOUR IDEA

Licensing right to manufacture product, based on your idea to a firm or corporation does not require as much money, but you still have to present your idea properly. If you are successful, next comes agreement(s) signing. So, you would need to spend money on attorney's services here as well.

Licensing comes in various shapes, so to speak. There is no rigid scheme, just many ways to approach the issue. Licensing may be exclusive and non-exclusive. "Exclusive" means, that you give right to manufacture to one company and agree not to sell license to anybody else, especially to this company's direct competitors. This agreement may be for certain number of years or forever or for the duration of the patent protection.

Licensing often means that you get paid a "lump sum" for your time and effort during development of your idea, sketches, drawings, models and prototypes. Plus, you will want to negotiate royalties, which may be anywhere between 1% and 15%, depending on many details, such as, field of your invention, market demand, potential returns, investment for manufacturing and so on.

SELL OR NOT TO SELL?

In many cases inventors choose to sell their invention outright. In most cases this is what buying party prefers. Many corporations prefer to buy the entire invention – patent, if it has already been issued, or right to patent, if invention is pending. This is one of the cases when Provisional Patent Application comes very handy and may help inventor to sell his idea. When invention is for sale, you still can ask for a lump sum to be paid and negotiate royalties. The difference is that inventor signs off his entire rights for his invention to the buying party. From that moment inventor is no longer the owner of the patent. His name will still be on the patent as "Inventor", but he will no longer own it.

I am often being asked by inventors during consultation meetings, if selling is good for them. In order to answer this question, I try to understand what inventor wants and what he is realistically capable to do. Can he or she afford manufacturing on their own? Would licensing be right? Why not to sell? I know inventors who were lucky to invent something once, sell it out right, retire to an exotic island and never worry about regular income again. Wouldn't that be nice? This is probably the ultimate wish and goal of most independent inventors.

PRESENTATION OF YOUR IDEA. TAKE IT SERIOUSLY

Whichever way you turn, looks like proper presentation is a key to moving forward towards success. So, what is this "presentation" I keep talking about? It may take many forms and you will have to choose the way you will present your idea depending on your talent to speak, ability to convince and sell, complexity of your idea itself and many other factors. You may try to manage with the same sketches and drawings, which were used in Provisional Patent Application and rich body language. But in many, if not most, cases this will not be enough.

You will need to research potential market, position your idea or product based on your idea in that market niche, understand what your potential buyers want and need and present your idea to them in a most attractive way, keeping these "want" and "need" aspects in mind. You will be presenting your idea to company managers, possibly to owners. These are usually business people and from my personal experience I learned, that CEOs, VPs, business managers and project managers are BUSINESS PEOPLE, even if some of them have education and experience in creative fields. And they will come with very limited, if any at all, imagination for this meeting with you. When it comes to evaluating novelty product idea, they make decisions based on numbers most of the time. On numbers and on what they see and can touch. This is unfortunate fact and you will have to deal with it. What it means is that more often than not these people see only what you bring to show and not what you try to explain and describe. If you come to the meeting with sketches, renderings, drawings and charts, prepare carefully and select proper sketches, drawings and renderings, which clearly show and explain your idea. Taking too little visual material is as bad as bringing too much of it. Try to minimize visuals, but make sure that you have enough to illustrate your concept, its novelty side and, what is most important, projected financial gains and revenue increases, which product, based on your idea will provide. These are such things as low manufacturing costs, high potential market demands and possibility of attractive mark up of the product in distribution and retail. Every company and corporation wants to gain reputation of innovative leader in their industries, but their ultimate goal is always going to be revenue and profit.

DO YOU REALLY NEED A PROTOTYPE?

The short answer to this will be, yes, in most cases working prototype is the best way to present your product idea. In some cases, this is the only way. Yes, it costs money to build one. Some inventors, especially handy ones, can build acceptable prototypes themselves, saving money in the process. Others will have to use services of model makers to do that. Unfortunately, it is getting increasingly hard to find good prototype maker in the USA and Canada these days. Many of them had to close businesses due to the fact that most companies build models and prototypes with potential manufacturers in China, India, Mexico and other countries, where cost of such services is cheaper.

Many design companies list prototyping as one of their services, but some of them will not take just prototype building task. They offer it as part of whole product development service.

I often receive phone calls from independent inventors asking if I could quote and build prototype for them. When they arrive for a meeting to my office, turns out they do not have anything except rough un-professional pencil sketch. Some of them get quite disappointed to learn that prototype or even mock-up model cannot be built from such sketch. No matter how brilliant inventor's idea may be, it still has to be turned into 3-D CAD model and 2-D dimensional drawing before it can be built as prototype.

Going back to prototyping process, once you reached that stage and made decision to build one, you can start searching for help by running "Prototyping Services" or "Prototyping Companies" string on Google. If you do not find anything nearby, then run a different search: "Product Design Companies" or "Industrial Design Firms" in your state. My strong advice is always to build prototypes with local service provider, who you can visit as often as necessary, to stay in control of the process and quality of your model fabrication.

WHAT IS NDA? DO YOU NEED TO HAVE ONE?

What is NDA and how much legal power does it have? NDA (Non-Disclosure Agreement) is a simple legal document, which you sign with someone before having discussion of your idea. It purpose is to protect you and your idea in cases, when you have no choice but to involve other individuals or companies in work on its development. NDA obliges the party, to which you release confidential and proprietary information, to keep and treat it as such and release it only to employees on a "need to know" basis. NDA may not be the armor for all and any situation, but as legal binding document, it does have power and it provides you with some level of protection and peace of mind. You can customize your NDA slightly, if needed, but be careful. Twisting NDA too much may turn some of its parts into those, "unenforceable" by law.

Always sign NDA first, before discussing your idea with anybody, asking for a quote or even small advice. You will find example of such NDA at the end of this book. Feel free to use it. You can also Google various NDAs. Make sure that it spells that you are the "Discloser" of proprietary information and that this NDA does not bind you as Discloser and Receiving Party in any way and does not give this party any authorship rights to intellectual property which you are about to share. Always put small standard "Confidentiality" disclosure in your emails, when you have discussions of your project. You may also insert "Confidential Information" line into subject of your emails and/or faxes. It is also advisable to have small marking or watermark "Confidential" is present on all sketches and drawings you send out.

FORMS AND EXAMPLES

NDA (Non-Disclosure Agreement):

CONFIDENTIALITY AND NON-DISCLOSURE AGREEMENT

This AGREEMENT is made this_____day of_____20_____,between

(First and last name)_____

of (Company name if any)_____,

located at (full address)_____

(hereinafter the "DISCLOSING PARTY")

And

(First and last name)_____

of (Company name if any)_____,

located at (full address)_____

(hereinafter the "RECEIVING PARTY").

Whereas DISCLOSING PARTY possesses certain PROPRIETARY INFORMATION relating to "product development concepts and designs, sales and marketing strategies, product pricing and sales results", which is desired to be disclosed to RECEIVING PARTY, this disclosure being for the purpose of evaluation thereof and, possibly, in regard to entering into a further agreement with DISCLOSING PARTY for the purpose of facilitating marketing and/or sale of products made based upon the PROPRIETARY INFORMATION detailed above, and possibly for further evaluation of said PROPRIETARY INFORMATION, said PROPRIETARY INFORMATION being hereby deemed to include all disclosures by DISCLOSING PARTY to RECEIVING PARTY of any type or format of information including but not limited to oral, written, graphic and/or machine recognizable disclosures as well as all samples, prototypes, models, drawings, sketches and/or individual parts thereof; and

Whereas RECEIVING PARTY agrees to receive this PROPRIETARY INFORMATION for the purpose of considering usage thereof, and for possibly advising concerning the manufacture and/or sale of certain items, prototypes, parts or products based on said PROPRIETARY INFORMATION;

NOW THEREFORE IT IS AGREED by and between both parties as follows:

1. RECEIVING PARTY agrees to maintain all PROPRIETARY INFORMATION in confidence and shall not disclose same to any third party nor make any use thereof in any manner whatsoever without prior written approval of DISCLOSING PARTY unless it can be proved with fully legally acceptable corroborative evidence that said PROPRIETARY INFORMATION:

    A. was already in the public domain at the time of execution of this AGREEMENT;

    B. becomes part of the public domain after execution of this AGREEMENT by publication or otherwise, from a source other than through RECEIVING PARTY.

    C. can be shown by RECEIVING PARTY with fully verifiable corroboration as having been in its possession at the time of signing of this AGREEMENT without having been acquired directly or indirectly from DISCLOSING PARTY; or

    D. comes to RECEIVING PARTY, independently, without binder of secrecy, subsequent to the execution of this AGREEMENT, from persons who receive such information neither directly nor indirectly from DISCLOSING PARTY.

2. DISCLOSING PARTY and RECEIVING PARTY mutually agree to maintain in confidence all discussions, determinations, findings and disclosures incident to this AGREEMENT or generated during performance hereunder.

3. RECEIVING PARTY agrees not to make any use of any of the PROPRIETARY INFORMATION disclosed under this AGREEMENT other than uses strictly necessary

and incident to the evaluation and consideration thereof in accordance with fulfilling the terms and purposes of this AGREEMENT.

4.   No rights to make use of said PROPRIETARY INFORMATION for any purpose whatsoever, other than as specifically set forth herein, are being conveyed by DISCLOSING PARTY under this AGREEMENT.

5.   RECEIVING PARTY agrees to limit disclosure of PROPRIETARY INFORMATION only to those employees and/or others who must be directly involved in this project and RECEIVING PARTY agrees to be responsible to assure that all parties receiving disclosure materials will comply with all terms and conditions of this AGREEMENT.

6.   The terms and conditions of this AGREEMENT shall apply to all subsidiaries, parent corporations, divisions, shareholders, partners and employees of both parties to this AGREEMENT as well as employees and/or others as detailed in Paragraph 5 above.

7.   At the time of termination of evaluation and consideration of the PROPRIETARY INFORMATION, RECEIVING PARTY agrees to return all disclosure materials received in accordance with performance under this AGREEMENT and all copies thereof including but not limited to all written, graphic and/or machine recognizable disclosures as well as all samples, prototypes, models, drawings, sketches and/or individual parts thereof.

8.   This AGREEMENT will remain in full force and effect for five years (60 months) from the date of execution of this AGREEMENT.

9.   This AGREEMENT shall inure to the benefit of and shall be binding upon the successors, assigns, and representatives of both parties hereto, and shall be construed in accordance with the laws of the State of New Jersey, USA.

IN WITNESS WHEREOF, the parties have executed or caused this AGREEMENT to be executed by their duly authorized representatives to become effective as of the date given above.

AGREED:

(Signature) _____   _____

for   DISCLOSING PARTY   DATE

(type name and address) _____

(Signature) _____   _____

for   RECEIVING PARTY   DATE

(type name and address) _____

CONFIDENTIALITY FOOTNOTE FOR EMAIL COMMUNICATIONS:

CONFIDENTIALITY NOTICE

The information contained in this communication is confidential information intended only for the use of the individual(s) or entities named above. If the reader of this communication is not the intended recipient, you are hereby notified that any copying, dissemination or distribution of this communication is strictly prohibited. If you have received this communication in error, please delete it immediately and notify us by telephone.

FORM PTO/SB/16 (PROVISIONAL PATENT APPLICATION COVER SHEET)

(PDF file can be downloaded from http://www.uspto.gov/sites/default/files/forms/sb0016.pdf)

Or from my blog website http://www.myinventionhub.com from "Useful Links" section.

PPA PATENT DRAWINGS AND REFERENCING EXAMPLE

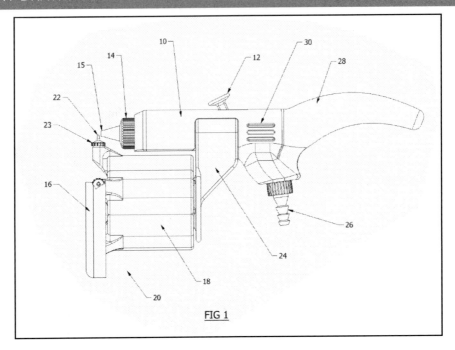

FIG 1

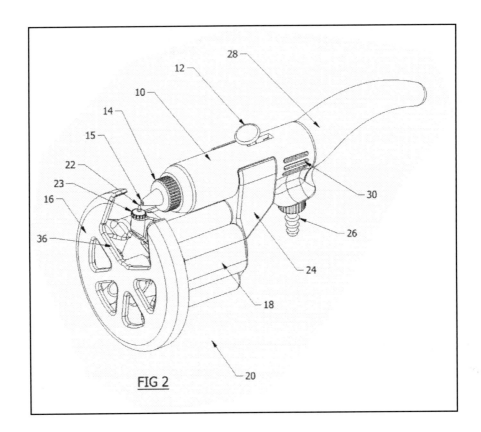

FIG 2

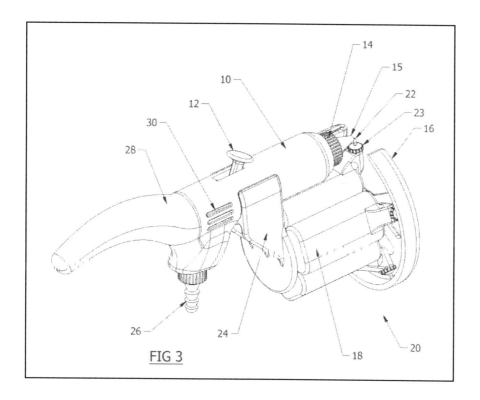

FIG 3

IN THE UNITED STATES PATENT AND TRADEMARK OFFICE

Utility Patent Application (Provisional)

Multi-Color Spraying Device

John Smith, Livingston, New Jersey

SPECIFICATION

CROSS-REFERENCE TO RELATED APPLICATIONS
Not Applicable

STATEMENT REGARDING FEDERALLY SPONSORED RESEARCH OR
DEVELOPMENT
Not Applicable

REFERENCE TO SEQUENCE LISTING, A TABLE, OR A COMPUTER PROGRAM
LISTING COMPACT DISK APPENDIX

Not Applicable

BACKGROUND OF THE INVENTION

The present invention is in the technical field of hand-held spraying devices. More particularly, the present invention is in the technical field of spraying liquids, such as paints, liquid cosmetic solutions or liquid medications.

Conventional spraying devices, such as hand-held airbrushes all require either to drain one color or liquid from the feeding tank before filling tank with a different color or liquid, or they require to detach used tank from the handle and attach another one. In both cases process of switching from one color/liquid to another requires initial spraying of new liquid content into an absorbing tissue or container to purge remnants of previously used color/liquid and avoid cross contamination between first and second color/liquid.

SUMMARY OF THE INVENTION

The present invention is a hand-held spraying device for users to instantly switch

between multiple colors or liquid types without any cross contamination of colors or liquid types and without need to ever drain and clean airbrush before, during or after use of airbrush.

BRIEF DESCRIPTION OF THE DRAWINGS

Fig. 1 is a side view of a spraying device of the present invention;

Fig. 2 is a forward perspective view of a spraying device of Fig. 1;

Fig. 3 is a backward perspective view of a spraying device of Fig. 1;

Fig. 4 is an exploded view of a spraying device of Fig. 1;

Fig. 5 is a side view of a spraying device version of present invention;

Fig. 6 is a forward perspective view of a spraying device of Fig. 5;

Fig. 7 is backward perspective view of spraying device of Fig. 5;

Fig. 8 is an exploded view of spraying device of Fig. 5;

Fig. 9 is an exploded view of multi-color cartridge of spraying device of Fig. 5;

DETAILED DESCRIPTION OF THE INVENTION

Referring now to the invention in more detail, in Fig. 1 there is shown an airbrush 10 having a handle 28, ergonomically curved for comfortable hold in a user's either right or left hand, main air nozzle 14 with its front tip 15, trigger 12, located approximately in the middle and top portion of handle 28, air venting holes 30, air inlet tube 26 and multi-color cartridge assembly 20. Multi-color cartridge 20 has a mainframe 24 and array of tanks 18, each of which hold liquid and/or colors. Mainframe 24 holds array of tanks 18, has front sealing ring 16 and attaches itself to the underside of the handle 28 using snapping feature 34 as shown in Fig. 4. Each of the tanks 18 has tank nozzle 22 with a ring for manual adjustment 23.

In further detail, still referring to the invention of Fig. 1; Fig. 2; Fig 3 and Fig.4, the array of tanks 18 of cartridge 20 can rotate around horizontal axel to provide instant switching between any of the tanks 18 for convenient and un-interrupted spraying of different colors without draining or cleaning tanks 18 or draining and cleaning of main nozzle 14 or tank nozzle 22.

The construction details of the invention are that the airbrush 10 may be made of injection plastic, such as ABS, or of any other sufficiently rigid and strong plastic material such as metal, and the like. Further, the various components of the airbrush 10 can be made also of plastic or metal or other materials.

Cartridge 20 has mainframe with snapping feature 34, which fixedly attaches to the recess 32 on the underside of airbrush handle 28. Mainframe 24 of cartridge assembly 20 stays in fixed position, while array of tanks 18 can rotate around horizontal axel of mainframe 24 with preset angles to provide precise positioning of tank nozzles 22 in front of airbrush nozzle 14 during each rotation.

Referring now to Fig. 4, there is shown exploded view of airbrush 10 having an air inlet tube 26 attaching to the underside of airbrush handle 28. Fig. 4 also shows sealing ring 16, which is attaching to the axel of cartridge mainframe 24 and provides sealing of liquid tanks 18 which are not currently in spraying position. Sealing ring 16 has V-shaped opening 36 in its upper portion, which allows spraying of content of the tank 18, which is positioned in spraying position in front of airbrush nozzle 14.

Airbrush handle 28 has air venting slots 32, which vent pressurized air, when trigger 12 is in forward non-spraying position. As trigger 12 is moved back towards the rear end of airbrush handle 28 pressurized air is redirecting itself and starts coming at high velocity through front tip 15 of airbrush nozzle 14.

In more detail, still referring to the invention of Fig. 1-4, the diameter of front tip 15 of airbrush nozzle 14 is greater than diameter of tank nozzle 22, which creates Venturi Effect during passing of high-velocity air from airbrush nozzle 15 over tank nozzle 22 and thus providing spraying effect.

As shown in Fig. 1, main nozzle 15 has serrations 14 on its base for ease of adjusting position of said nozzle 15 in horizontal direction and in that fashion controlling distance between main nozzle 15 and tank nozzle 22, which allows to control width of spraying angle. Tank nozzle 22 also has serrations 23, allowing to rotate said nozzle 22, and elevate or lower down its position in relation to main nozzle 15, which provides control of spray density.

The construction details of the invention as shown in Fig. 4 are that the cartridge 20 can be easily and instantly disengaged from airbrush handle 28 and replaced with another cartridge 20, that contains a set of other liquids or colors. For example, cartridge with all neon paint can be instantly replaced with cartridge containing all pastel colors. Or, cartridge with all warm grayscale colors can be instantly replaced with cartridge holding all cold gray-scale colors.

Referring now to Fig. 5, there is shown an airbrush 40 having a multi-color cartridge 50 with array of liquid tanks 48, assembled around vertical axel of cartridge mainframe 52, which attaches itself to the lower portion of airbrush 40.

In further detail, referring to the invention of Fig. 5-9, the color cartridge 50 contains a sealing ring 46, which seals nozzles of tanks 48 not in use. Tanks 48 are positioned vertically and rotating around vertical axel of mainframe 52 of cartridge 50, allowing easy access to any of the tanks 48 for immediate spraying without draining or cleaning.

The construction details of the invention as shown in Fig. 8 are that the handle 40 has cutout area on its bottom section to accommodate attaching cartridge 50 using snapping feature 56 and positioning sealing ring 46 in such a way, that V-shaped opening 58 of sealing ring 46 will face forward and provide enough open space for spraying of the content of tank 48, currently positioned in front of airbrush nozzle 44.

Referring now to Fig. 8, there is shown an airbrush 40 with its handle 62, having a recess feature 66, onto which cartridge snaps with its snapping feature 56 into a fixed position.

Referring to Fig.9, there is shown exploded view of the multi-color cartridge 50, having

mainframe 52 and top sealing ring 46, array of liquid color tanks 48. Color tanks assemble around stem 74 of the mainframe 52, attaching themselves to the stem 74 radially. Each liquid color tank 48 has protruding upper steel button 70 and protruding lower steel button 72, used for precise positioning of said color tank 48 into assembly of cartridge 50. Stem 74 of the cartridge mainframe 52 has recessed openings 76 in its upper section and similar openings 78 in lower section, which correspond in shape and spacing to steel buttons 70 and 72 on each tank. Liquid color tank 48 can easily be positioned precisely into the cartridge 50 by means of either plastic snaps or by using small round magnets, recessed into openings 76 and 78 on the mainframe stem 74.

Mainframe 52 is constructed in such fashion that its bottom platform, holding tanks 48 can rotate around centerline of stem 74 in incremental angles, providing snapping stop points at such precise angles, so as to position any of the tanks 48 precisely in front of airbrush nozzle 44.

As shown in Fig. 5, main nozzle 44 has serrations 43 on its base for ease of adjusting position of said nozzle 44 in horizontal direction and in that fashion controlling distance between main nozzle 44 and tank nozzle 54, which allows to control width of spraying angle. Tank nozzle 54 also has serrations, allowing to rotate said nozzle, and elevate or lower down its position in relation to main nozzle 44, which provides control of spray density.

The advantages of the present invention include, without limitation, that it provides easy and instant access to multiple colors without need for draining or cleaning. Present invention provides un-interrupted flow of work. Current invention makes it exceedingly easy to switch between number of colors within one cartridge and/or switch between different cartridges, containing different types of liquids.

In broad embodiment, the present invention is an airbrush containing multi-color cartridge with horizontal or vertical axel of tanks rotation.

While the foregoing written description of the invention enables one of ordinary skill to make and use what is considered presently to be the best mode thereof, those of ordinary skill will understand and appreciate the existence of variations, combinations, and equivalents of the specific embodiment, method, and examples herein. The invention should therefore not be limited by the above described embodiment, method, and examples, but by all embodiments and methods within the scope and spirit of the invention as claimed.

ABSTRACT OF THE DISCLOSURE

A spraying device has multi-color cartridge with horizontal axel of cartridge rotation.

And

A spraying device has multi-color cartridge with vertical axel of cartridge rotation.

OTHER GREAT SOURCES OF INFORMATION

- **"Protect Your Great Ideas For Free!"** book by attorney J. Nevin Shaffer, Jr., Esq., $29.95 paperback from Amazon.com or Kindle version for $26.95

- **"Sell Your Ideas With or Without A Patent"** book by Stephen M. Key and Janice Kimball Key $17.59 paperback from Amazon.com or Kindle version for $15.95

- **"The Inventor's Complete Handbook: How to Develop, Patent, and Commercialize Your Ideas"** book by James L. Cairns; $19.95 paperback or $19.95 for Kindle version from Amazon.com

- **"Patent Your Idea"** by Ash Tankha; $29.99 paperback from Amazon.com or $8.99 Kindle edition.

- **"Patent It Yourself"** by David Pressman and Thomas J. Tuytschaevers $37.48 paperback from Amazon.com or $28.99 Kindle edition

- **"Profit From Your Idea: How to Make Smart Licensing Deals"** by Richard Stim; $83.36 for paperback from Amazon.com

- **"How to Make Patent Drawings: A Patent Yourself Companion"** by Jack Lo and David Pressman; paperback $8.99

READER RESPONSE AND REVIEWS

If you purchased, read and tried to use this book, I would like to hear your comments, questions and suggestions. This is the first edition of my book and I hope to keep improving it, adding new information based on current developments in patent laws and processes. But I also want to know readers' opinion. Please, send them to info@myinventionhub.com or leave a comment on my website www.myinventionhub.com in Contact section.

Made in the USA
Monee, IL
05 October 2020